KINGDOM EQUIPMENT 101

KINGDOM EQUIPMENT 101

TOOLS FOR KINGDOM PURPOSE

TERRY STEPHENS

J MERRILL

J Merrill Publishing, Inc.
434 Hillpine Drive
Columbus, OH 43207
www.JMerrill.pub

Library of Congress Control Number: 2023902739
ISBN-13: 978-1-954414-77-8 (Paperback)
ISBN-13: 978-1-954414-76-1 (eBook)

Book Title: Kingdom Equipment 101
Author: Terry Stephens
Cover Artwork: Safeer Ahmed

CONTENTS

INTRODUCTION

Kingdom Equipment 101 is one of several textbooks for our Kingdom Equipment Ministry Business Academy. It is a Bible-centered training program designed to establish believers in biblical principles for ministry and business for those seeking to achieve tangible growth and results from their obedience to God. K.E.M.B.A is an equipping ministry resource used to help individuals discover their purpose, define their calling, and become equipped to do all that God has created them to do. With a systematic approach to measuring growth, students will develop knowledge, skill, and practical application in assembly and marketplace ministry. In addition, K.E.M.B.A. provides valuable opportunities in and out of the classroom environment for students to develop their gifts, skills, systems, methods, and principles.

K.E.M.B.A. is training focused on the model of Jesus training his disciples over three years. During this time, Jesus taught Kingdom principles, demonstrated Kingdom authority, and gave practical, real-life opportunities for his disciples to practice with his oversight. This course is action-packed with hands-on training, homework, practical teachings, and activations in and out of the classroom to help students find, understand and walk in their Kingdom assignment with confidence, skill, and character. We will cover subjects like servant leadership, spiritual authority, knowing your calling, marketplace ministry, God's business plan, operating in the supernatural, engaging your natural & spiritual gifts, team ministry & the fivefold ministry gifts, and much more.

We're equipping the found to preach to the lost!!!!!!!!

K.E.M.B.A. includes education but is more training focused.

Training	Education
Pursuit of Ability	Pursuit of Knowledge
Improves Performance and Productivity	Develops a Sense of Reasoning and Judgment
Method of Skill Development	Method of Gaining Knowledge
Teaches Certain Skills	Teaches General Concepts
Practical Application	Theoretical Orientation
Short-Term Process	Long-Term Process
Narrow Scope	Wide Scope
Related to Employment	General Learning
Prepares for Present Job	Prepares for Future Jobs

SMART KPI's							
Specific, Measurable, Attainable, Realistic Time-bound Key Performance Indicators							
Covenant	Dispensation	Rank	Ministry	Age	Fruit	Gifts	Ethics
Edenic	Innocence	PVT	New Convert	Infant	Love	Wisdom	Diligence
Adamic	Conscience	PFC	Kingdom Citizen	Toddler	Joy	Knowledge	Knowledge
Noahic	Human Gov't	SPC	Deacon	Preschool	Peace	Faith	Knowledge
Abrahamic	Promise	SGT	Minister	School Child	Longsuffering	Healing	Temperance
Mosaic	Law	SSG	Elder	Adolescent	Gentleness	Miracles	Patience
Palestian	Grace	SFC	Overseer	Young Adult	Goodness	Prophecy	Godliness
Davidic	Kingdom	MSG	Pastor	Middle Adult	Faith	Discernment	Brotherly Love
New Covenant	Eternal State	CSM	Bishop	Adult	Meekness	Tongues	Charity
Measuring Growth Through Systemic Theology							
This is not doctrine but a parallel of things to measure progress, advancement, and fruitfulness.							

We are using the dispensations & covenants, military rank system, ministry titles, and Erik Ericksons developmental psychology analysis on human development as growth indicators and goals to reach toward and the spiritual gifts, fruit of the Spirit, and 2 Peter ethics that make you fruitful as KPI's (key performance indicators). Our goal is to challenge believers to measure their growth. This is systematic theology that we don't consider doctrine, but we'll use to manage growth toward leadership and fruitfulness. With so many leaving the church in this generation, we believe it's our responsibility to show practical and tangible ways the church adds value to people's lives besides good music and an encouraging word on Sundays.

The first words of God to mankind were about work. The last words of Jesus to his disciples were about work. The scripture says the harvest is plenteous, but the laborers are few.

As you learn and become familiar with the equipment God has given you.

LET'S GET TO WORK.

Every employer provides their employees with everything needed to accomplish the task. The employee is responsible for familiarizing themselves with the equipment given and using it to accomplish their goals. In these books, you'll discover that God has done the same for us. He has given us all things that pertain to life and godliness. I call them Kingdom Equipment. Our responsibility is to familiarize ourselves with the equipment and learn to use it to fulfill our purpose.

Consider these scriptures

> *According as his divine power <u>hath</u> given unto us all things that pertain unto life and godliness, through the knowledge of him that hath called us to glory and virtue: 4Whereby are <u>given</u> unto us exceeding great and precious promises: that by these ye might be partakers of the divine nature, having escaped the corruption that is in the world through lust. 5And beside this, giving all diligence, add to your faith virtue; and to virtue knowledge; 6And to knowledge temperance; and to temperance patience; and to patience godliness; 7And to godliness brotherly kindness; and to brotherly kindness*

charity. 8For if these things be in you, and abound, they make you that ye shall neither be barren nor unfruitful in the knowledge of our Lord Jesus Christ. 9But he that lacketh these things is blind, and cannot see afar off, and hath forgotten that he was purged from his old sins. 10Wherefore the rather, brethren, give diligence to make your calling and election sure: for if ye do these things, ye shall never fall:

— (2 PETER 1:3-10 KJV)

Blessed be the God and Father of our Lord Jesus Christ, who <u>hath</u> blessed us with all spiritual blessings in heavenly places in Christ:

— (EPHESIANS 1:3 KJV)

But as it is written, Eye <u>hath</u> not seen, nor ear heard, neither have entered into the heart of man, the things which God <u>hath prepared</u> for them that love him. But God <u>hath revealed</u> them unto us by his Spirit: for the Spirit searcheth all things, yea, the deep things of God.

— (1 CORINTHIANS 2:9-10 KJV)

Friends, God has equipped us with all the Kingdom Equipment we need to fulfill our purpose successfully.

THE DISPENSATION OF INNOCENCE AND THE EDENIC COVENANT

Dispensationalism is a systematic way of understanding the Scriptures in a progressive yet extensive way—and thus informs us how we are to serve the Lord during a particular time in which we live.

> *16For though I preach the gospel, I have nothing to glory of: for necessity is laid upon me; yea, woe is unto me, if I preach not the gospel!*
>
> *17 For if I do this thing willingly, I have a reward: but if against my will, a dispensation of the gospel is committed unto me.*
>
> *18 What is my reward then? Verily that, when I preach the gospel, I may make the gospel of Christ without charge, that I abuse not my power in the gospel.*
>
> — (I COR 9:16-18)

> *That in the dispensation of the fulness of times he might gather together in one all things in Christ, both which are in heaven, and which are on earth; even in him:*

— (EPHESIANS 1:10)

If ye have heard of the dispensation of the grace of God
which is given me to you-ward:

— (EPHESIANS 3:2)

Whereof I am made a minister, according to the
dispensation of God which is given to me for you, to
fulfill the word of God;

— (COLOSSIANS 1:25)

A new dispensation begins when a new revelation or instructions given by God is revealed. This new revelation or understanding of things changes mankind's relationship and responsibility to God and the rest of mankind. Caution neither a better understanding of the text nor a fulfillment of prophecy, by itself, initiates the beginning of a dispensation. But a new dispensation comes with a significant change in the instructions of mankind for a particular time.

Covenant theology views all of scripture under God's one purpose, which is the salvation of mankind.

Dispensational theology views Scripture under a broader purpose: the restoration of God's purpose for creation.

A revelation is a disclosure of truth, instruction, manifestation, appearance,

Consider this concerning Adam and Eve.

> *When the woman saw that the tree was good for food and*
>   *pleasing to the eyes, and that it was desirable for*
>   *obtaining wisdom, she took the fruit and ate it. She also*
>   *gave some to her husband who was with her, and he*
>   *ate it.*
> *And the eyes of both of them were opened, and they knew*
>   *that they were naked; so they sewed together fig leaves*
>   *and made coverings for themselves.*
>
> — (GENESIS 3:6,7)

Adam and Eve received a revelation from their disobedience by eating the fruit, changing how God related to them. This revelation ushered them from the dispensation of innocence to the dispensation of conscience. God now had to relate to them based on their conscience instead of their innocence. Asking them where are you? He asks Eve What is this that thou hast done? Then he proceeds to distribute the changes to the assignment that was initially given. But because they got this revelation due to disobedience, they must complete the assignment the hard way now.

Later in our studies, we will discuss the other revelations that adjusted and changed dispensations throughout history.

- Innocence—the dispensation of the Garden of Eden
- Conscience—the dispensation from the fall to the flood
- Human Government—the dispensation from the flood to the promise of a nation through Abraham
- Promise—the dispensation from Abraham to Moses
- Law—the dispensation from Moses to Paul
- Grace—the dispensation from Paul to the fullness of time
- Kingdom—the dispensation from the second coming of Christ to the New Heavens and New Earth.

Dispensation	Covenant
Innocence	Edenic
Sonscience	Adamic
Human Government	Noahic
Promise	Abrahamic
Lay	Mosaic
Grace	Palestian
Kingdom	Davidic
Eternal State	New Covenant

Genesis chapters 1-3 tells us God didn't create Adam only to lounge in a beautiful garden. Instead, He gave him specific instructions with measurable outcomes. This contract between God and Adam is the first covenant between God and any man, commonly known as the Edenic Covenant. Adam becomes God's first independent contractor. In this covenant, God supplied Adam with many blessings: life, a perfect body, a perfect environment, a world without pain, hunger, sickness, or death, and a wife. All Adam (and Eve) had to do was fulfill six instructions God had laid down to keep the covenant in effect with all its blessings. God told them to:

1. Be fruitful, multiply, and replenish the earth (Gen. 1:28).
2. Subdue the earth for their use (Gen. 1:28).
3. Exercise dominion over the animal creation (Gen. 1:28).
4. Have only a vegetable diet (Gen. 1:29).
5. Dress and keep the garden they were put in (Gen. 2:15).
6. Abstain from eating from the Tree of Knowledge of Good and Evil (Gen. 2:17).

A Covenant is an agreement, contract, or compact between two or more parties.

Knowing and understanding the details of every assignment, revelation, or instruction from God is important. Unfortunately, the details of this assignment came into question and were the subject of their temptation.

We must obey God circumspectly, carefully, and prudently. God is very detailed in his instructions, and we must abide by them with the same attention to detail.

> *And the LORD God took the man and put him into the garden of Eden to dress it and to keep it. And the LORD God commanded the man, saying, Of every tree of the garden thou mayest freely eat: But of the tree of the knowledge of good and evil, thou shalt not eat of it: for in the day that thou eatest thereof thou shalt surely die.*
>
> — (GEN. 2:15-17)

> *And when the woman saw that the tree was good for food, and that it was pleasant to the eyes, and a tree to be desired to make one wise, she took of the fruit thereof, and did eat, and gave also unto her husband with her; and he did eat.*
> *And the eyes of them both were opened, and they knew that they were naked; and they sewed fig leaves together, and made themselves aprons.*
> *And they heard the voice of the Lord God walking in the garden in the cool of the day: and Adam and his wife hid themselves from the presence of the Lord God amongst the trees of the garden.*
> *And the Lord God called unto Adam, and said unto him, Where art thou?*

> *And he said, I heard thy voice in the garden, and I was*
> *afraid, because I was naked; and I hid myself.*
> *And he said, Who told thee that thou wast naked? Hast*
> *thou eaten of the tree, whereof I commanded thee that*
> *thou shouldest not eat?*
>
> — (GEN 3:6-11)

The first temptation of man had to do with food- the forbidden fruit – and the first temptation of Jesus had to deal with was food – turning stones into bread (Luke 4:3). Our appetites are Satan's favorite playground. He tempted Eve with all three categories of temptation the world has to offer:

1. The lust of the flesh
2. The lust of the eyes
3. The pride of life (I John 2:16)

> *Eve saw the tree, she took of the fruit, and did eat. As is*
> *usually the case – others are affected by their own sin –*
> *she gave to Adam and "he did eat"*
>
> — (GENESIS 3:6)

This is the natural progression of temptation leading to sin:

> *"Let no man say when he is tempted, I am tempted of God:*
> *for God cannot be tempted with evil, neither tempteth*
> *he any man: But every man is tempted, when he is*
> *drawn away of his own lust, and enticed. Then when*
> *lust hath conceived, it bringeth forth sin: and sin, when*
> *it is finished, bringeth forth death"*
>
> — (JAMES 1:13-15)

Sin automatically uncovered them. The penalty for their sin went into effect immediately. It didn't wait for their day in the courts of heaven. God told them they would surely die in the day they ate from the tree of good and evil.

In the same way, your unforgiveness locks your forgiveness.

> *For if ye forgive men their trespasses, your heavenly Father will also forgive you: But if ye forgive not men their trespasses, neither will your Father forgive your trespasses.*
>
> — (MATTHEW 6:14-15)

For the wages of sin is death, but the gift of God is eternal life through Jesus Christ our Lord.

What really happened when Adam and Eve disobeyed God's command? God had warned that disobedience would result in death. But did Adam instantly fall dead? No, he lived to the age of 930 years. Yet man DID die the very moment he ate the forbidden fruit. Since man is a spirit-being, it was into the spirit, created in God's Image, that death entered. This does not mean that Adam and Eve ceased to be spirit-beings. Rather than being a state of non-existence, spiritual death is an existence separated and alienated from God.

Three kinds of death are mentioned in Scripture:

Physical death – separates man's spirit and soul from his body.

Spiritual death – separates man's spirit from God.

Second death – is an eternal separation of man from God whereby God's Nature is never again accessible (Revelation 20:11-15).

Man also experienced physical death. The Bible says that Adam lived to be 930 years old. So we know he didn't physically die instantly. But he did still die a physical death in that day.

> *But, beloved, be not ignorant of this one thing, that one*
> *day is with the Lord as a thousand years, and a*
> *thousand years as one day.*

— (2 PETER 3:8)

930 years is 70 years shy of 1000 years, which equates to a day with God.

Spiritual death is as real as life. The difference is that death comes from Satan and life from God. All that is good, beautiful, and holy originates from God. All that is evil, bad, and corrupt comes from the Devil. Satan's nature began to rule in the spirit of man when spiritual death seized dominion over creation.

> *"..by one man's offence death reigned... by one man's*
> *disobedience many were made sinners.. sin hath reigned*
> *unto death.."*

— (ROMANS 5:17, 19, 21)

We understand from God's Word that man is three-fold: spirit, soul, and body.

- The spirit is the real inner man, the part that knows God.
- The soul is the mind (or intellect), the will and emotions that operate by the five senses of seeing, hearing, touching, tasting, and smelling.
- The body is the house or building where the invisible spirit and soul live.

But here's the good news. First, we must read the whole scripture.

*For if by one man's offence death reigned by one; much
more they which receive abundance of grace and of the
gift of righteousness shall reign in life by one, Jesus
Christ.) Therefore, as by the offence of one judgment
came upon all men to condemnation; even so by the
righteousness of one the free gift came upon all men
unto justification of life. For as by one man's
disobedience many were made sinners, so by the
obedience of one shall many be made righteous.
Moreover the law entered, that the offence might
abound. But where sin abounded, grace did much more
abound: That as sin hath reigned unto death, even so
might grace reign through righteousness unto eternal
life by Jesus Christ our Lord.*

— (ROM 5:17-21)

DISCUSSION TOPIC #1

Mankind's assignment

Why do you think God created the heavens and earth and mankind? Why do you think God wants you in the Kingdom? What was your reason for joining the Kingdom?

John 15:16 – You didn't choose me, I chose you
John 6:44 – No man comes to me unless the father who sent me draws

Discussion tips:

We were created to advance and rule God's Kingdom on earth.

Is it possible our reason for getting saved and God's reason for saving us are most likely different?

Understanding that God chose us and we didn't choose him, we need to find out what he chose us for. Again, Jeremiah 29:11 speaks of God having plans for us.

What do you think God's plan is for your life? Are you willing to live out that plan?

DISCUSSION TOPIC #2

EMPOWERMENT

What does it mean to be blessed? Why did God bless them? Why do you think God has blessed you? Gen 2:28 And God blessed them.

You were blessed to be a blessing. Gen 12

Christ has blessed us in the heavenly realms with every spiritual blessing. Eph 1:3

His divine power has given us everything we need for life and godliness through our knowledge of him who called us by his own glory and goodness. 2 Peter 1:3

Are you blessed for your own happiness or for the benefit of the Kingdom?

What am I blessed (empowered) to do? Jesus used James and John's natural occupation to advance the Kingdom. Can what you do naturally be used to advance the Kingdom spiritually? Matt 4:18, 19; Rom 12:6

DISCUSSION TOPIC #3

FOUNDATION OF THE FAMILY

According to Genesis 1:28, what is man's purpose? What is the woman's purpose? How does the woman's purpose connect to the purpose of the man?

Discussion topics: God has never cut a covenant with anyone without giving instructions. Adam's relationship with God was based on the mission.

Before interviewing potential helpmeets, a man should have three things: home, resources, and mission.

A woman should be suitable (compatible) and well able to help with the mission before marriage. (Genesis 2:18-20)

The purpose of mankind is to help God advance his Kingdom on earth. The woman's purpose is to help man help God. Therefore, as the man submits to God, so should the woman submit to man to accomplish the mission God has given. The foundation and purpose of marriage are not about emotional love, houses, cars, and land. It is about accomplishing the will of God on the earth. Emotional love, houses, cars, and land are included but are not the family's foundational purpose.

CHAPTER NOTES

_____

_____

_____

_____

_____

_____

_____

_____

_____

_____

_____

_____

_____

_____

_____

_____

_____

_____

_____

_____

_____

_____

_____

_____

_____

_____

_____

_____

_____

_____

_____

_____

_____

_____

_____

_____

FAMILY FIVEFOLD MANDATE

God's original intent was never to have a bunch of churches, denominations, fellowships, etc., that all operated, believed, and lived differently. God's original plan was to have a Kingdom on earth that he would rule over through the spirits of men. With the Kingdom mindset, we understand that Kingdoms don't expand or advance by individual aspiration. Kingdoms advance through colonization.

When speaking in terms of colonization, I'm not referring to legalism and tradition. Instead, I'm suggesting that God fully intended for the kingdom to operate and function like a kingdom governmentally, economically, and socially.

The foundation of God's business plan to build, maintain, and advance his Kingdom was to put a man and a woman in a structured garden with specific instructions.

> *Then God said, "Let us make mankind in our image, in our*
> *likeness, so that they may rule over the fish in the sea*
> *and the birds in the sky, over the livestock and all the*
> *wild animals, and over all the creatures that move*
> *along the ground."*
> *So God created mankind in his own image, in the image of*
> *God he created them; male and female he created them.*
> *God blessed them and said to them, "Be fruitful and*
> *increase in number; fill the earth and subdue it. Rule*
> *over the fish in the sea, the birds in the sky, and every*
> *living creature that moves on the ground."*
>
> — (GENESIS 1:26-28) NIV

Man was created in God's image to express his desire for family. The image of God is the identity of the Kingdom. Without his image, he is unrecognizable in the lives of his people.

> *For whom he did foreknow, he also did predestinate to*
> *be conformed to the image of his Son, that he might be*
> *the firstborn among many brethren.*
>
> — (ROMANS 8:29) KJV

See, God already had Jesus in mind, even in the beginning. Jesus was meant to be the firstborn of many brethren. Jesus was the first human to participate in the renewed opportunity to be a part of God's family through Salvation. He was our example.

But notice in Genesis 1 that he blesses them first, meaning he empowered them. This is significant because it speaks of our need for the power of the Holy Spirit.

Then he gave the first family a fivefold mandate:

- Be Fruitful
- Multiply
- Replenish the earth
- Subdue it
- Have Dominion

These five instructions represent God's business plan for our families. These instructions exemplify the goal of building, maintaining, and advancing the family.

Before we go further into the fivefold mandate, let's look at the structure of the family.

According to Genesis, we see a threefold foundational leadership structure.

God, Adam, and Eve. They represent the Prophet, Priest, and King model throughout the Old and New Testaments as God's foundational leadership structure. God as King, Adam as the Prophet, and Eve as the Priest.

Prophet	Priest	King
Adam	Eve	God
Moses	Aaron	God
Samuel	Ahimelech	Saul
Samuel/Nathan	Zadok	David
Nathan	Azariah	Solomon

As you can see, this structure continued throughout the whole Old Testament.

In the New Testament, you see this structure of team ministry continue. In the gospels, Jesus always sent the disciples out two by two. He was the 3rd chord.

> *Calling the Twelve to him, he sent them out two by two and gave them authority over evil spirits.*

> — (MARK 6:7)

In Ephesians 2:19, 20

> *Consequently, you are no longer foreigners and strangers, but fellow citizens with God's people and members of his household, built on the foundation of the apostles and prophets, with Christ Jesus himself as the chief cornerstone.*

More on that later.

So, God with Adam and Eve represents our foundational leadership structure with a fivefold mandate to:

Be fruitful
Multiply
Replenish the earth
Subdue it
Have Dominion

The family was the first institution to be introduced to God's business plan using the fivefold mandate.

More on the fivefold mandate later. Let's look at two popular words that many get confused about.

Purpose and destiny are not the same things. Destiny speaks to who you become, while purpose speaks to what you accomplish for God.

(Destiny) For whom he did foreknow, he also did
predestinate to be conformed to the image of his Son,
that he might be the firstborn among many brethren.

— (ROMANS 8:29) KJV

(Destiny) (Purpose) And God said, Let us make man in our
image, after our likeness: and let them have dominion
over the fish of the sea, and over the fowl of the air, and
over all the earth, and over every creeping thing that
creepeth upon the earth.

— (GENESIS 1:26)

(Destiny) But as many as received him, to them gave he
power to become the sons of God, even to them that
believe on his name.

— (JOHN 1:12)

Therefore, understanding the difference between purpose and destiny is important. First, let's look at the sequence of events.

1. God makes man in his image (destiny) - God is a spirit, so man is made in the spirit first; we don't see man's body come into the picture until Genesis.
2. God then gives man his purpose. (The fivefold mandate)
3. After accepting the mandate, mankind is then exposed to the resources God has given to sustain them while on assignment.

All of this is in Genesis chapter 1. Mankind had not even been given a body yet.

In Genesis chapter 2 is where mankind is now given a body from the dust of the ground and put in the garden of Eden, where they are expected to fulfill the purpose given to them.

Adam & Eve had a threefold assignment.

1. The fivefold mandate
2. Dress and keep the garden
3. Don't eat of the tree of knowledge of good and evil.

What has God assigned you to?

What has he told you not to do?

What are some of the convictions the Holy Spirit has highlighted to you?

What details are important to you?

You must know and understand these details so that you don't miss an important part while fulfilling the fivefold mandate.

Consider the following as God's business plan, the fivefold mandate.

Church	Tabernacle	Garden	Business
Evangelists	Brazen Altar	Be Fruitful	Recruiters
Teachers	Brazen Laver	Multiply	Trainers
Pastors	Tablel of Shewbread	Replenish	Supervisor
Prophets	Golden Candlesticks	Subdue	Advisors
Apostles	Altar of Incense	Dominion	Administrators

These gifts don't define who a person is; they define the area where a person functions on the team.

Friends, your family is your business. God will give you the assignment for your family to complete. It is your job to fulfill your purpose (the fivefold mandate) while pursuing and developing in the destiny (image) God gave you.

In Genesis 2, God forms man physically and puts them in the garden to dress and keep it. He then says it's not good for man to be alone and vows to make him a helper.

The job of Eve is to help Adam with the purpose and destiny God gave him.

The children come, and they should be immediately introduced to the assignment.

CHAPTER NOTES

_____

_____

_____

_____

_____

_____

_____

_____

_____

_____

_____

_____

_____

_____

_____

_____

_____

_____

_____

_____

_____

_____

_____

_____

_____

_____

_____

_____

_____

_____

_____

_____

_____

_____

_____

_____

_____

_____

_____

_____

_____

_____

_____

_____

ORIGINAL YOU

F riends, in this hyper-prophecy generation, it's important to understand the basics of prophecy. Especially to those who don't know who they are and what their assignment is on the earth. In order to really be about God's business, we must know who we are, our purpose, and what gifts we've been given to accomplish that purpose.

Understanding that, we must start where God starts. Who we are in God's eyes starts in the beginning.

> *Before I formed thee in the belly I knew thee; and before*
> *thou camest forth out of the womb I sanctified*
> *thee, and I ordained thee a prophet unto the nations.*
>
> — JEREMIAH 1:5 KJV

Friends, your destiny started in God's mind before you were born. Before you were hurt, traumatized, sick, etc., your life had been planned out. Before you discovered your gifts and developed a reputation based on your performance in life, God had a plan for your life.

Jeremiah 29:11 says

> For I know the plans I have for you, declares the LORD,
>   plans to prosper you and not to harm you, to give you a
>   future and a hope.

To understand who you are, you must begin your search in the mind of God at the beginning.

With the beginning in mind and the prophetic view of your destiny, we must also consider this verse.

> (As it is written, I have made thee a father of many
>   nations,) before him whom he believed, even God, who
>   quickeneth the dead, and calleth those things which be
>   not as though they were.

> — (ROM 4:17)

The word were, is a verb second person singular past, plural past, and past subjunctive of be.

So, if prophesy is forth-telling, according to this scripture, prophecy is telling forth from the past.

Everything God thinks or thought about you was done in the beginning. Here are a few scriptures to consider.

> According as his divine power hath given unto us all things
>   that pertain unto life and godliness, through the
>   knowledge of him that hath called us to glory and
>   virtue: Whereby are given unto us exceeding great and
>   precious promises: that by these ye might be partakers

of the divine nature, having escaped the corruption that
is in the world through lust.

— (2 PETER 1:3,4)

Blessed be the God and Father of our Lord Jesus Christ, who
    hath blessed us with all spiritual blessings in
    heavenly places in Christ: According as he hath chosen
    us in him before the foundation of the world, that we
    should be holy and without blame before him in love:
    Having predestinated us unto the adoption of children
    by Jesus Christ to himself, according to the good
    pleasure of his will, To the praise of the glory of his
    grace, wherein he hath made us accepted in the beloved.

— (EPH 1:3-6)

And we know that all things work together for good to them
    that love God, to them who are the called according
    to his purpose. For whom he did foreknow, he also did
    predestinate to be conformed to the image of his Son,
    that he might be the firstborn among many brethren.
    Moreover whom he did predestinate, them he also
    called: and whom he called, them he also justified: and
    whom he justified, them he also glorified.

— (ROMANS 8:28-30)

Understanding the finished works of Christ is vital to the prophetic and how it is ministered. So many prophesy that God is getting ready to do this and getting ready to do that. So language proves they don't understand the scriptures and the formula for the manifestation of the things of God. Consider this scripture.

But as it is written, Eye hath not seen, nor ear heard,
neither have entered into the heart of man, the things
which God hath prepared for them that love him.
But God hath revealed them unto us by his Spirit: for the
Spirit searcheth all things, yea, the deep things of God.

— (1 CORINTHIANS 2:9, 10)

Everything God planned for us was designed in the beginning and revealed to us by the Holy Spirit.

If you can't hear from God through the Holy Spirit, how
will you know what to ask him for. If he doesn't reveal
to you what he's prepared for you, you will continue ask
based on your own lust and not according to his will.

— (REF JAMES 4:3)

The hand of the LORD was upon me, and carried me out in
the spirit of the LORD, and set me down in the midst of
the valley which was full of bones, And caused me to
pass by them round about: and, behold, there were very
many in the open valley; and, lo, they were very dry.
And he said unto me, Son of man, can these bones live?
And I answered, O Lord GOD, thou knowest. Again he
said unto me, Prophesy upon these bones, and say unto
them, O ye dry bones, hear the word of the LORD.
Thus saith the Lord GOD unto these bones; Behold, I
will cause breath to enter into you, and ye shall live:
And I will lay sinews upon you, and will bring up flesh
upon you, and cover you with skin, and put breath in
you, and ye shall live; and ye shall know that I am the
LORD.
So I prophesied as I was commanded: and as I prophesied,
there was a noise, and behold a shaking, and the bones

came together, bone to his bone. And when I beheld, lo,
the sinews and the flesh came up upon them, and the
skin covered them above: but there was no breath in
them. Then said he unto me, Prophesy unto the wind,
prophesy, son of man, and say to the wind, Thus saith
the Lord GOD; Come from the four winds, O breath,
and breathe upon these slain, that they may live. So I
prophesied as he commanded me, and the breath came
into them, and they lived, and stood up upon their feet,
an exceeding great army.

Then he said unto me, Son of man, these bones are the
whole house of Israel: behold, they say, Our bones are
dried, and our hope is lost: we are cut off for our parts.
Therefore prophesy and say unto them, Thus saith the
Lord GOD; Behold, O my people, I will open your
graves, and cause you to come up out of your graves,
and bring you into the land of Israel. And ye shall know
that I am the LORD, when I have opened your graves,
O my people, and brought you up out of your graves,
And shall put my spirit in you, and ye shall live, and I
shall place you in your own land: then shall ye know
that I the LORD have spoken it, and performed it, saith
the LORD.

— (EZEKIEL 37:1-14)

In vs 5, Ezekiel begins his prophecy by causing the breath to enter the bones. This is interesting because when God created, he also started with the spirit. Then he goes to the sinews. A sinew is a piece of tough fibrous tissue uniting muscle to bone or bone to bone; a tendon or ligament. And finally, he adds flesh to the bones and sinews. So the soul is made up of the mind, will, and emotions. But also, the body is made up of bone, sinews, and flesh. So indeed, a three-fold cord is not easily broken.

So is Ezekiel a doctor to know the chronological order this prophecy must go in? There's no evidence of that. But clearly, he understood something about the way this needed to happen. I believe God gave him the orderly arrangement of how these were living men before and the instructions to resurrect them.

In vs. 7, we see a picture of Pentecost. The scripture says there was a noise, and behold a shaking, and the bones came together, bone to his bone.

The Pentecost scripture is very similar.

> *And suddenly there came a sound from heaven as of a rushing mighty wind, and it filled all the house where they were sitting.*
>
> — (ACTS 2:2)

Pentecost demonstrates the power of Jesus' death, burial, and resurrection as the Holy Spirit begins his role of resurrecting mankind from the spiritual death created by Adam and Eve.

CHAPTER NOTES

_____

_____

_____

_____

_____

_____

_____

_____

_____

BIBLE STUDY TIPS

When approaching the bible for study, it is important to understand that God and his word are one. So we should always pray and ask God to help us to understand his word. In addition, I always ask him to reveal to me his current thoughts concerning a particular text.

We should never approach the Word of God with preconceived ideas.

Two distinctions concerning God's word are vital to proper studying.

Rhema word – living spoken word, spiritual Logos – the living written word, natural

Note: YOU CAN NOT LIVE OFF JUST THE WRITTEN WORD OR THE WORD OF YOUR SPIRITUAL LEADER

> *But he answered and said, It is written, Man shall not live by bread alone, but by every word that proceedeth out of the mouth of God.*

— (MATTHEW 4:4)

Jesus replied, "Blessed are you, Simon son of Jonah, for this was not revealed to you by man, but by my Father in heaven. And I tell you that you are Peter, and on this rock I will build my church, and the gates of Hades will not overcome it. I will give you the keys of the kingdom of heaven; whatever you bind on earth will be bound in heaven, and whatever you loose on earth will beg loosed in heaven."

— (MATTHEW 16:17-19)

Faith comes by hearing, not reading. Reading confirms what you hear from the Holy Spirit.

Grammar and punctuations matter. Words like but, for, that, whosoever, whatsoever, wherefore, and therefore matter. I often use the thesaurus for synonyms to ensure I get the correct context or use of the word.

Let's use John 3:16 as a case study.

For God so loved the world, that he gave his only begotten Son, that whosoever believeth in him should not perish, but have everlasting life.

Things to consider when looking at this particular scripture.

The word For - could be substituted with because Loved – is used in the past tense.

World – Greek definition is orderly arrangement Because God so loved the orderly arrangement

Now I must visit Genesis Ch. 1 to study and understand the orderly arrangement for which he gave his only begotten son.

Look at Philippians 4:15-19

A famous quote that we often use about God supplying our needs: but when you look at this in the context in which it was written, this quote should not be spoken for personal use. Paul declared this prophetically over the Philippians because they had given to him even when he wasn't with them.

To understand the context in which scripture is being written, it is suggested to read the whole chapter before, the chapter you are focusing on, and the chapter following.

Who was the writer?

Who was the writer writing to?

What was the dominant culture of the people?

How does this relate to Jesus and the death, burial, and resurrection?

Resources to use:

- Different versions of the Bible
- Dictionary
- Thesaurus
- Strong's Concordance
- Bible Dictionary
- And most of all, the Holy Spirit

NO SCRIPTURE STANDS ALL BY ITSELF

Four different men wrote the gospels about the same accounts. The prophets prophesied many of the same things and confirmed other prophets' words.

Allow God to confirm your revelation through the word and by the words of spiritual leaders.

CHAPTER NOTES

_____

_____

_____

_____

_____

_____

_____

_____

_____

_____

_____

_____

_____

_____

_____

_____

_____

_____

_____

_____

_____

_____

_____

_____

_____

_____

KEY PERFORMANCE INDICATOR CHALLENGE (KPI)

DILIGENCE, LOVE, WORD OF WISDOM

What is a KPI? A quantifiable measure of performance over time for a specific objective. KPIs provide targets to shoot for, outcomes to achieve, and milestones to gauge progress.

Students must set goals for themselves in operating these spiritual tools (diligence, love, word of wisdom) to make progress.

Journal about the journey, the struggle, the triumph, the ups and downs, failure, and success. But also how your progress using this equipment is helping you move closer to your goals and developing your spiritual power.

Send weekly updates on how these spiritual tools are helping them.

DILIGENCE CHALLENGE

Success and failure, many times, comes down to one missing link. It's not that others are more talented, gifted, favored, etc. It's not about resources, where a person comes from, or how they grew up. It's not even that God is a respecter of persons. The scriptures clearly express that God is not.

For there is no respect of persons with God.

— (ROMANS 2:11)

The missing link can often be found in one word: diligence. If we look up "diligence" in a dictionary or thesaurus, it is defined. Persevering application. Assiduousness. Industriousness. Vigor. Care. Diligence is an attitude that drives us to accomplish a mission successfully. In other words, diligence is the opposite— the extreme opposite—of laziness.

The whole book of Proverbs explains and illustrates the concept of diligence. Proverbs is a practical manual for success. Each proverb relating to diligence shows the difference between failure and success —between missing the mark and achieving the goal.

> *The lazy man does not roast what he took in hunting, But diligence is man's precious possession.*
>
> — (PROVERBS 12:27 NKJV)

> *Lazy people don't even cook the game they catch, but they diligently use everything they find.*
>
> — (PROVERBS 12:27 NLT)

What good is it to go grocery shopping but never cook the food? You still end up eating out. Diligence is about finishing what we start.

> *"He becometh poor that dealeth with a slack hand: but the hand of the diligent maketh rich.*
>
> — (PROVERBS 10:4 ERV)

> *He who has a slack hand becomes poor, But the hand of the diligent makes rich.*
>
> — (PROVERBS 10:4 NKJV)

A slack hand is a lazy hand—an uncooperative hand. Laziness leads to poverty. On the other hand, if you are diligent and actively cooperate with God, you help yourself to riches.

God's job is to secure the inheritance; our job is to go get it from the wicked.

He who gathers in summer is a wise son; He who sleeps in harvest is a son who causes shame.

— (PROVERBS 10:5 NKJV)

A wise youth harvests in the summer, but one who sleeps during harvest is a disgrace.

— (PROVERBS 10:5 NLT)

God will not reap your harvest for you. His job is to increase the seed. That's why the scripture says the harvest is plenteous, but laborers are few.

— (LUKE 10:2)

In all labor there is profit, But idle chatter leads only to poverty.

— (PROVERBS 14:23 NKJV)

Work brings profit, but mere talk leads to poverty!

— (PROVERBS 14:23 NLT)

Don't talk about it, be about it.

Here are other scriptures on diligence.

Hebrews 11:6 – Proverbs 13:4 – Hebrews 6:11 – 2 Peter 1:10 – Proverbs 22:29

Proverbs 4:23 - Proverbs 12:24 – 2 Peter 3:14 – Deut 4:9 – 1 Tim 4:15 NIV

LOVE CHALLENGE

*Jesus said unto him, thou shalt love the Lord thy God with
all thy heart, and with all thy soul, and with all thy
mind. This is the first and great commandment. And the
second is like unto it, thou shalt love thy neighbor as
thyself. On these two commandments hang all the law
and the prophets.*

— (MATTHEW 22:37-40 KJV)

I often wondered why the order was to love God first, then love my neighbor as myself. Until I got the revelation, wait a minute, if God is love, then I can't love others if I don't love God. And I have to have God to love him too. So receiving Christ as my Lord and Savior not only gives me remission of sin, it now affords me the love I need to love God, others, and myself. Accepting God's love for me helps me understand how he made me, the good, bad, and ugly, and how he loves everything I don't like or love about myself and understands how to adjust those things to make them lovable.

Beloved, let us love one another: for love is of God; and every one that loveth is born of God, and knoweth God. 8He that loveth not knoweth not God; for God is love. 9In this was manifested the love of God toward us, because that God sent his only begotten Son into the world, that we might live through him. 10Herein is love, not that we loved God, but that he loved us, and sent his Son to be the propitiation for our sins. 11Beloved, if God so loved us, we ought also to love one another. 12No man hath seen God at any time. If we love one another, God dwelleth in us, and his love is perfected in us. 13Hereby know we that we dwell in him, and he in us, because he hath given us of his Spirit. 14And we have seen and do testify that the Father sent the Son to be the Saviour of the world. 15Whosoever shall confess that Jesus is the Son of God, God dwelleth in him, and he in God. 16And we have known and believed the love that God hath to us. God is love; and he that dwelleth in love dwelleth in God, and God in him. 17Herein is our love made perfect, that we may have boldness in the day of judgment: because as he is, so are we in this world. 18There is no fear in love; but perfect love casteth out fear: because fear hath torment. He that feareth is not made perfect in love. 19We love him, because he first loved us. 20If a man say, I love God, and hateth his brother, he is a liar: for he that loveth not his brother whom he hath seen, how can he love God whom he hath not seen? 21And this commandment have we from him, That he who loveth God love his brother also.

— (1 JOHN 4:7-21)

Then in 1 Corinthians 13, we get more details about how love works and how we are to love God, ourselves, and others. But many have taught this chapter about loving others when it is really about loving yourself.

> *Charity suffereth long, and is kind; charity envieth not; charity vaunteth not itself, is not puffed up, Doth not behave itself unseemly, seeketh not her own, is not easily provoked, thinketh no evil; Rejoiceth not in iniquity, but rejoiceth in the truth; Beareth all things, believeth all things, hopeth all things, endureth all things. Charity never faileth: but whether there be prophecies, they shall fail; whether there be tongues, they shall cease; whether there be knowledge, it shall vanish away.*
>
> — (1 CORINTHIANS 13:4-8 KJV)

> *And now abideth faith, hope, charity, these three; but the greatest of these is charity.*
>
> — (1 CORINTHIANS 13:13 KJV)

Friends, love comes with the Holy Spirit. It is a part of the fruit of the Spirit. Therefore, it is at your disposal at all times. Nothing you do can be done outside of the love of God.

After you've learned how God loves you and experienced his love for you, you now have an example of how to love yourself and others. But there's another level.

How do I express or display God's love toward others?

> *Having then gifts differing according to the grace that is given to us, whether prophecy, let us prophesy according to the proportion of faith; Or ministry, let us wait on our ministering: or he that teacheth, on teaching; Or he that exhorteth, on*

exhortation: he that giveth, let him do it with
simplicity; he that ruleth, with diligence; he that
sheweth mercy, with cheerfulness. Let love be without
dissimulation. Abhor that which is evil; cleave to that
which is good.

— (ROMANS 12:6-9 KJV)

Verse 9 sums up all of these gifts with love, which means that using the gifts God has given you for the benefit of others is operating in the love of God.

Friends, one last thing about love that you must know and understand. Love is the prescription for fear. What do you mean? If you're dealing with fear, God's answer to ridding yourself of fear is love.

There is no fear in love; but perfect love casteth out fear:
because fear hath torment. He that feareth is not made
perfect in love.

— (1 JOHN 4:18 KJV)

No more praying to God to help you overcome your fear. Love is a part of the fruit of the Spirit. It's in you; it just needs to be activated. When you immerse yourself in the love of God through the word of God, fear cannot exist in the same space.

Always remember, God won't do for us what he's already equipped us to do for ourselves. For example, God has equipped every believer with love to deal with fear.

WORD OF WISDOM CHALLENGE

B ecause of how I've been trained, it can be challenging to teach about the word of wisdom without the other two revelation gifts, the word of knowledge and prophecy. But to be simple and practical about the word of wisdom, it is simply put, the wise instruction necessary to see the will of God come to pass in a person's life.

Wisdom is different from knowledge. Wisdom is directive or applicable, whereas knowledge is informative.

When wisdom is given, it is for the proper application of knowledge. With this understanding, I often use instruction as my word to explain what the word of wisdom does. Wisdom is about action. The Bible says that wisdom is the principal thing; therefore, get wisdom.

> *Wisdom is the principal thing; therefore get wisdom: and with all thy getting get understanding.*

> — (PROVERBS 4:7 KJV)

If any of you lack wisdom, let him ask of God, that giveth to all men liberally, and upbraideth not; and it shall be given him.

— (JAMES 1:5 KJV)

An example of a word of wisdom is when Joseph interpreted the dream of Pharoah and instructed him to store up food for seven years.

We will teach more about this later when we discuss spiritual gifts.